About the Painting

As a young boy I remember the experience of seeing a Norman Rockwell painting entitled *The Land of Enchantment*, which illustrated a youthful girl and boy lounging in the foreground reading books, with a parade of storybook characters marching along in the background. It is a remarkable visual demonstration of how the power of the written word can stimulate our minds and imaginations. It is a painting that I have always remembered.

A Father's Heritage is the result of my long felt desire to create a painting in a similar fashion, but one that is based on the precept of a father reading God's Word to his own children. If we look beyond the obvious warmth and intimacy of the moment, we see illustrated a far more important event in the lives of the children and the father. The father is fulfilling his role as the one who is responsible to introduce his children to the Word of God. As the Holy Spirit empowers the reading of the Word, it touches the hearts of his son and daughter, and their youthful imaginations come alive. The seed of the Word is planted into fertile ground, and the Lord now has the opportunity to make the seed grow in His time, bearing the fruit of God's Spirit.

"Tell it to your children, and let your children tell it to their children,
and their children to the next generation."
JOEL 1:3
"Hear ye sons, the instruction of a father, and attend to know understanding."
PROVERBS 4:1

This painting addresses the need of our children today to know about God's love for them and the Judeo-Christian foundation upon which they can base their lives. It is the responsibility of all of us, particularly as parents, to make sure that our children grow up with a love and a respect for what God says, and to know that, in life, the Bible is our greatest source of wisdom, comfort, and joy. The lives of the hundreds of characters that fill the Bible, a few of which are illustrated here, bring this Word to life and help make it so relevant to parents, their children, and their children yet to come.
I know firsthand the impact that a beautiful painting can have on a child. If, years ago, Rockwell's art inspired me to read about cowboys and Indians, swashbucklers, and Huck Finn, then I have to believe that art inspired by God's Holy Spirit can draw people to the reading of His Word. My prayer is that God would use *A Father's Heritage* for just such a purpose.

C. MICHAEL DUDASH

NOTES ABOUT THE PAINTING: *"A Father's Heritage" is an oil painting executed on linen mounted on a gatorfoam panel - 35"h x 48"w. Friends, family, and yours truly posed for the various characters.*

FURTHER NOTE: *I have had some comments from people asking about the absence of the mother in the painting. I chose to restrict this particular setting to just the father because of the great need I see in our contemporary society for him to reassume his role as the spiritual leader of his children. This is not meant to imply that the mother is any less important. Indeed, it is all too often that it is the mother or the single mother that has to take on this responsibility. The role she plays as a spiritual example and teacher is equally necessary. A future painting may well address this subject.*

Foreword

Spiritual heritage, passed from parent to child, can have a life changing impact on a child. Michael Dudash, was prompted to create the painting *A Father's Heritage* after experiencing first hand the powerful influence a picture can have on the life of a child. Michael's faith comes through in the scene depicted in the painting. As the father reads the stories, he brings the Bible to life in the minds of his children. This powerful book is the result of that rich heritage of faith that was passed to the author, Roy Lessin, from his father, Joseph. Roy has used his faith to be an influence, not only on the lives of his children and grandchildren, but also on countless others through his writings.

I was taught the value of a Christian heritage through a Bible that has been passed down in our family for generations. My ancestors' hand written inscriptions in that Bible illustrate a desire to share with their children their belief in God's Word. From my grandfather, to my father, on to me, and to my son and grandson—the spiritual heritage continues. From the personal reflections passed on in our family Bible, the idea for this book began. To that idea, the creative art direction of Todd Knowlton was added, and that concept became the book you hold in your hand. It is a beautiful expression of God's truth that will allow parents the opportunity to teach their children and share their faith.

As Christian fathers, these men are uniquely suited to combine their gifts in *A Father's Heritage*. It is easy to see their love for the Lord Jesus expressed through their work. It is my prayer that this book will enable Christian parents to share their heritage for generations to come.

ROGER W. TROVER

Dedication

Dedicated to my two beautiful granddaughters, Grace and Andrea—with a prayer that I will always be faithful to pass on to you the rich heritage of faith that I have received from my father and your great grandpa, Joseph.

With thanks to my two children, Joey and Lydia, whose lives are testimonies to the faithfulness of God in their generation.

With deepest gratitude to my wife, Charlene, who for 33 years has lovingly given to me and our family the priceless heritage of a Christian wife and mother.

ROY LESSIN

THE FAITHFULNESS OF GOD—FROM GENERATION TO GENERATION

A Father's Heritage
THE PAINTING BY C. MICHAEL DUDASH

"We will not hide them from their children;
we will tell the next generation the praiseworthy deeds of the Lord,
His power, and the wonders He has done."
PSALM 78:4

WRITTEN BY ROY LESSIN

THE MasterPeace
COLLECTION
A Division of DaySpring® Cards

A Father's Heritage

THE PAINTING BY C. MICHAEL DUDASH
WRITTEN BY ROY LESSIN

FIRST EDITION
©1998 BY THE MASTERPEACE® COLLECTION
A DIVISION OF DAYSPRING® CARDS.
ALL RIGHTS RESERVED

ORIGINAL CONCEPT/FOREWORD: ROGER W. TROVER

ART DIRECTION: TODD C. KNOWLTON

BOOK DESIGN: MOE STUDIO INC.

17602

PRINTED IN HONG KONG

ISBN: 1-884009-75-1

Contents

How To Use This Book

"For everything that was written in the past was written to teach us, so that through endurance and the encouragement of the Scriptures we might have hope."

ROMANS 15:4

This is a book for you to read to your children—but more than a story book, it is designed to be a keepsake, passed on from generation to generation. It is a book to fathers and for fathers. The book is designed to teach, build faith, create interest, promote conversation, and prompt questions. It is a book of celebration and participation.

The book goes beyond the characters and events of the Bible stories that are shown in the painting. The book goes to the heart of the story—to share principles of faith and obedience, God's heart and God's ways, and the rich meaning of the Christian heritage that has been passed on from generation to generation. It is a book to ponder, to read, to study, and to enjoy.

Each chapter is based on a Bible character or event that is featured in the backdrop of the painting, *A Father's Heritage*. Each chapter includes a narrative of the specific Bible story that is illustrated, a devotional reflection based upon the story, additional Scriptures on the chapter's theme, and a special "Heritage Page" for a father to complete in his own words. Do not feel that you have to fill in these pages in one sitting, or in one year. Your entries can be recorded over the years as God continues to teach you and do new things in your life. The purpose of these pages is to help you show your children that the God who once walked with those in the Bible, also walks with you, and will walk with them. Each time you make an entry you will be passing on to your children and grandchildren a valuable keepsake of their spiritual heritage—a heritage they have received from your personal journey of faith.

A Father's Heritage brings to us a powerful lesson that impacts the life of a father and his children. In the painting, as the father gathers his children close and reads to them, their minds create the images that are shown in the backdrop of the painting.

In the left-hand corner of the painting, the children see Jesus in a way that is similar to the way they see their father. When the children's minds form a picture of Jesus, the image of their earthly father is clearly seen. The hands of Jesus reach out to bless in the same way that they see their father reaching out in blessing.

Children first learn the meaning of fatherhood through their earthly father. They can be introduced to the character of God through the character they see in their father, and they can learn about the heart of God when it is expressed through the heart of their father. What a beautiful picture this is, and what a great encouragement it provides to fathers who desire to leave a spiritual heritage to their children.

THE VALUE OF A FATHER'S HERITAGE

A man's commitment to God

The Heritage of Scripture

"Listen, my sons, to a father's instruction; pay attention and gain understanding. I give you sound learning, so do not forsake my teaching. When I was a boy in my father's house, still tender, and an only child of my mother, he taught me and said, 'Lay hold of my words with all your heart; keep my commands and you will live.' "

PROVERBS 4:1-4

"As a father has compassion on his children, so the LORD has compassion on those who fear Him."

PSALM 103:13

"Fathers, do not exasperate your children; instead, bring them up in the training and instruction of the Lord."

EPHESIANS 6:4

"Train a child in the way he should go, and when he is old he will not turn from it."

PROVERBS 22:6

" '...But as for me and my household, we will serve the LORD.' "

JOSHUA 24:15

" 'All your sons will be taught by the LORD, and great will be your children's peace.' "

ISAIAH 54:13

" 'For I have chosen him, so that he will direct his children and his household after him to keep the way of the LORD by doing what is right and just, so that the LORD will bring about for Abraham what He has promised him.' "

GENESIS 18:19

" 'Only be careful, and watch yourselves closely so that you do not forget the things your eyes have seen or let them slip from your heart as long as you live. Teach them to your children and to their children after them.' "

DEUTERONOMY 4:9

" 'Fix these words of Mine in your hearts and minds; tie them as symbols on your hands and bind them on your foreheads. Teach them to your children, talking about them when you sit at home and when you walk along the road, when you lie down and when you get up. Write them on the doorframes of your houses and on your gates, so that your days and the days of your children may be many in the land that the LORD swore to give your forefathers, as many as the days that the heavens are above the earth.' "

DEUTERONOMY 11:18-21

ne of the greatest gifts we can leave our children is a spiritual heritage. When we look back on our lives, we discover that our sweetest memories and richest treasures are found in the things that God has done for us. We recall our joys and remember how good He was… we recall our tears and remember how comforting He was… we recall our shortcomings and remember how merciful He was… we recall our fears and remember how loving He was… we recall our trials and remember how caring He was.

It is the faithfulness of God to us, in all the issues of life, that provides the eternal riches of a spiritual heritage. It is this heritage that will help our children understand and appreciate the values we carry, the faith we hold, and the hope we cherish in our hearts.

"Know therefore that the LORD your God is God; He is the faithful God,
keeping His covenant of love to a thousand generations
of those who love Him and keep His commands."
DEUTERONOMY 7:9

Deuteronomy 7:9

The Meaning of a Father's Heritage

From the beginning, the family was God's idea. God created the first man, Adam, and the first woman, Eve. He brought them together to live in a covenant relationship as husband and wife. This was a good relationship, a right relationship, a loving relationship, and a committed relationship. This was God's perfect plan and pattern for a family. Out of this relationship children were to be born, provided for, protected, nurtured, guided, trained, and loved. The presence of God and the love of God were to be the foundations of a family's heritage. God knew that people must first be rightly related to Him, before they could be rightly related to each other.

God has placed man as the leader of the family. It is to be a place of servant-leadership. In order for a father to have proper authority in His home, he first needs to submit himself to God's authority in his life. It is important for a man to do this, because he needs to learn from God, how to be a loving leader. As a father, a man is to nurture and train his children through his words and his example.

One of the things that God has always desired is to be glorified in a family, and through the lives of those within a family. When a conductor leads a symphony orchestra to play the music by a great composer, his goal is to present the beauty of the music that was created. Each member of the orchestra diligently trains and practices to accomplish this goal. It is the commitment of both the conductor and the musicians that makes this goal possible. When the goal is achieved, the impact upon an audience is tremendous, and is accompanied by ovation and appreciation. Through the presentation of the orchestra, the composer's work has been honored and praised. In the same way, through the commitment of a Christian father and his family, others can see the wonderful work God created when He formed the family. This faith commitment to God and to His plan is the basis of a father's heritage, and through it God is glorified.

"The boundary lines have fallen for me in pleasant places;
surely I have a delightful inheritance."
PSALM 16:6

Psalm 16:6

A Man's Commitment to God

I am a man, I am committed to be everything God intended for me to be when He made me a man—in will, mind, and emotions; in spirit, soul, and body; in purpose, strength, and character.

I am a man, I am steadfast even if others I meet may reject my faith, ridicule my convictions, question my sincerity, belittle my beliefs, or laugh at my loyalty.

I am a man, I stand with others that share a common bond in Jesus Christ, that desire to walk in right paths, that call upon God in sincerity and truth, and that seek to glorify Him at work and in the home.

I am a man, I care for the needs of my family, and I'm concerned about the needs of others. I care for my family by being there for them, by providing for them materially, and by ministering to them spiritually—humbly, gently, lovingly, and prayerfully.

I am a man, I am a servant to those that God has given me the responsibility to lead, to those I work with at the office, to those I labor with in the church, and to those I call loved ones or friends.

I am a man, I choose to live what I believe, whatever the cost, regardless of the situation, in season and out of season—because when I live what I believe it puts conviction in my words, integrity in my character, validity in my convictions, and truth in my heart.

I am a man, I am dependent on God's grace, on the Holy Spirit's power, on the blood of Jesus Christ, on the support and prayers of others, and on the fellowship of the body of Christ.

What Is A Man?

A MAN IS NOT A...

...stone, but bread that has been broken.

...fortress impenetrable, but a river of kindness and compassion.

...tower of steel, but a growing tree that provides covering and bends in the storm.

...ruler, but a servant who humbly seeks the success of others.

...sign-post, but a guide who leads through example.

...sculptor, but a gardener who nurtures and provides an atmosphere for growth.

...statue, but a communicator who speaks from the heart.

A MAN IS NOT AN ISLAND BUT A BRANCH, TOTALLY DEPENDENT UPON THE LIVING GOD!

God keeps
His promises

The Heritage of Scripture

" 'I have set My rainbow in the clouds, and it will be the sign of the covenant between Me and the earth.' "

GENESIS 9:13

"Not one of all the Lord's good promises to the house of Israel failed; every one was fulfilled."

JOSHUA 21:45

" 'Now Lord, God of Israel, keep for your servant David my father the promises you made to him when you said, "You shall never fail to have a man to sit before me on the throne of Israel, if only your sons are careful in all they do to walk before me as you have done." ' "

I KINGS 8:25

" 'My God is my rock, in whom I take refuge, my shield and the horn of my salvation. He is my stronghold, my refuge and my savior....' "

II SAMUEL 22:3

" 'Is not my house right with God? Has He not made with me an everlasting covenant, arranged and secured in every part? Will He not bring to fruition my salvation and grant me my every desire?' "

II SAMUEL 23:5

"Sing to the Lord, all the earth; proclaim His salvation day after day."

I CHRONICLES 16:23

"The salvation of the righteous comes from the Lord; He is their stronghold in time of trouble."

PSALM 37:39

" '...It is by the name of Jesus Christ of Nazareth, whom you crucified but whom God raised from the dead, that this man stands before you healed... Salvation is found in no one else, for there is no other name under heaven given to men by which we must be saved.' "

ACTS 4:10-12

"I am not ashamed of the gospel, because it is the power of God for the salvation of everyone who believes: first for the Jew, then for the Gentile."

ROMANS 1:16

" '...Believe in the Lord Jesus, and you will be saved—you and your household.' "

ACTS 16:31

*L*ong ago, the people who lived on the earth were of full of every kind of evil. The evil saddened God's heart. God was going to bring His judgement on this evil, by sending a great flood that would cover the earth and destroy every living thing upon it. But in His judgement, God also had mercy. God found a man whose heart trusted in Him, and who lived in a way that pleased God. The man's name was Noah. God spoke to Noah and told him about the judgement that was coming. God also told Noah that if he followed His instructions, Noah and his family could be saved from the coming flood.

Noah listened to God and followed God's instructions. God told him to build a giant boat—one as tall as a four story building, and longer than a football field. The boat was called the Ark. It took faith to build the Ark because Noah did not live by the ocean or a lake. Noah knew that when the boat was completed it would sit on dry ground, and that it would never float unless the flood came. It also took faith because Noah had to gather all the food for the animals and store it in the Ark. Noah knew that God would have to send him the animals because there was no way he could ever gather them all by himself.

By faith, and in obedience to God, Noah and his family started building the Ark. It would be a long, slow process. Many, many, years passed. Through Noah, God was extending His mercy to those outside of Noah's family. Because of God's great mercy, He was not in a hurry to judge the world for its great evil. He waited while Noah built the Ark. He waited while Noah's life and words warned others of the flood to come. He waited for anyone that would listen and turn to Him. But, in all that time, no one listened to God's words, no one paid any attention to His warnings, and no one wanted to turn away from evil.

One day, the Ark was finished. The time for the flood had come. Noah, his family, and all the animals entered the Ark. God closed the door of the Ark and sealed them inside. On that very day the flood began. Water came from everywhere—from above the ground and from below the ground. It continued for forty days and nights. The judgement upon evil was complete, but Noah and all those inside the Ark were saved.

When the flood ended, and all aboard the Ark returned to dry ground, Noah did a beautiful thing. He built an altar to God. On this altar he made a sacrifice, and gave God worship and thanks. What Noah did was like a sweet smelling fragrance to God, sweeter than the smell of a thousand roses. After God received the offering, He made a covenant with Noah, and blessed him and his family greatly.

Based on Genesis 6-9

God never makes a promise He can't keep. He can keep His promises because He has the power to do what He promises…because He doesn't change His mind about what He has promised…because He has the wisdom to know how to do what He has promised…and because He never forgets what He has promised.

God wants us to be so certain of His promises that He puts them in a binding agreement, called a covenant. Nothing can break God's covenant promises—they are unshakable, unbendable and unmovable. A covenant is like God saying to us, "I am not only giving you My promise, but I am also giving you a sealed oath that I will never break My promises to you."

God's most important promise, the one that brings Him the greatest joy to keep, is His promise to save us. The story of Noah, is the story of God's judgement on sin, and of His mercy to save those who have faith in Him. Noah was a righteous man, even though others didn't want to live the way God commanded them. He was an obedient man, even though others refused to listen to God's voice. He was a trusting man, even though others doubted God's word. Noah was a man who saw God keep His promises.

In every detail of Noah's story we see God's faithfulness. God told Noah how to build the ark, promising him that it would be the perfect size to carry his family, the animals, and their food—and it was; God said that He would send a flood to cover the earth—and He did; God told Noah and his family that the four seasons would continue on the earth—and they have; God placed a rainbow in the sky to remind us that He would never again destroy the earth by water—and He hasn't.

Before God judged the world with a flood, He told Noah to build a giant ship. This ship would become an ark of salvation for Noah and his family. God's promise to save us is found in Jesus Christ. Jesus is our ark of salvation. There is enough room in His heart to love each one of us…there is enough strength in His arms to hold each one of us…there are enough resources in His hands to care for each one of us. He is the perfect Saviour. He took our judgement for sin when He died for us on the cross, and He made a way for us to have new life when He rose from the dead. When we ask Jesus to forgive us, He does; when we ask Him to come into our hearts, He comes; when we trust Him to guide our lives, He leads us into everything that's good and right.

God Keeps His Promises

Personal Heritage Page

RECALLING GOD'S FAITHFULNESS IN MY LIFE
FOR MY CHILDREN AND GRANDCHILDREN TO ALWAYS REMEMBER.

The story of how God saved me:

_____

_____

_____

_____

_____

_____

_____

Date: _____

_____

_____

_____

_____

_____

_____

Date: _____

Date:

Date:

" So the next generation would know them, even the children yet to be born, and they in turn would tell their children. Then they would put their trust in God and would not forget His deeds but would keep His commands."

PSALM 78:6-7

God uses
ordinary things and ordinary
people

The Heritage of Scripture

"But Moses said to God, 'Who am I, that I should go to Pharaoh and bring the Israelites out of Egypt?' And God said, 'I will be with you….' Moses said to the Lord, 'O Lord, I have never been eloquent, neither in the past nor since you have spoken to your servant. I am slow of speech and tongue.' The Lord said to him, 'Who gave man his mouth? Who makes him deaf or mute? Who gives him sight or makes him blind? Is it not I, the Lord? Now go; I will help you speak and will teach you what to say.' "

EXODUS 3:11-12, 4:10-12

"Then the Lord said to Moses…'Tell the Israelites to move on. Raise your staff and stretch out your hand over the sea to divide the water so that the Israelites can go through the sea on dry ground.' "

EXODUS 14:15-16

" 'No one will be able to stand up against you all the days of your life. As I was with Moses, so I will be with you; I will never leave you nor forsake you.' "

JOSHUA 1:5

"When the angel of the Lord appeared to Gideon, he said, 'The Lord is with you, mighty warrior.' 'But Lord,' Gideon asked, 'how can I save Israel? My clan is the weakest in Manasseh, and I am the least in my family.' "

JUDGES 6:12, 15

"Although I am less than the least of all God's people, this grace was given me: to preach to the Gentiles the unsearchable riches of Christ."

EPHESIANS 3:8

"For the foolishness of God is wiser than man's wisdom, and the weakness of God is stronger than man's strength. But God chose the foolish things of the world to shame the wise; God chose the weak things of the world to shame the strong. He chose the lowly things of this world and the despised things—and the things that are not—to nullify the things that are, so that no one may boast before Him."

I CORINTHIANS 1:25, 27-29

"As He went along, He saw a man blind from birth. 'While I am in the world, I am the light of the world.' Having said this, He spit on the ground, made some mud with the saliva, and put it on the man's eyes. 'Go,' He told him, 'wash in the Pool of Siloam' (this word means Sent). So the man went and washed, and came home seeing."

JOHN 9:1, 5-7

any years after Jacob and his sons moved to Egypt, a new Pharaoh came into power. His heart was against the Hebrew people that now occupied his land and he was hard on them, making them into slaves and treating them with cruelty. One day his heart became so cruel that he commanded that all the Hebrew baby boys born in Egypt be killed. It was at that time that a Hebrew woman, with faith in God, put her young son in a floating basket, placing it in a safe, sheltered spot by the river's edge. She did this believing that God would send someone to rescue the child and care for him. To the mother's delight, her son was not only found, but she was asked to come and help care for him.

The baby was found by the daughter of Pharaoh, and she named him Moses. He grew up in the house of the most powerful family in all of Egypt. He learned everything there was to learn from the best teachers in the land, but Moses would later discover that God had lessons to teach him that were far greater than the ones he learned in Egypt.

One day Moses saw a Hebrew slave being mistreated by an Egyptian. He attacked the Egyptian and killed him. When Moses found out that Pharaoh knew what he had done, he fled Egypt. He lived a quiet life for many years as a simple shepherd. After forty years, God knew that Moses' heart was ready to learn new things. After God appeared to him, He sent Moses back to Egypt as the one He would use to deliver the Hebrew people from the cruelty of Pharaoh.

Through Moses, God sent ten great plagues upon Egypt. The plagues came because Pharaoh refused to let the Hebrew people leave his land. After the tenth plague, Moses and the Hebrew people finally were allowed to leave. But Pharaoh's heart was hard, and he decided to chase after the Hebrew people and bring them back—Pharaoh never learned that you can't fight against God and win. Pharaoh chased them all the way to the Red Sea, and there he and his entire army were drowned.

After this, Moses and the Hebrew people wandered in the desert for many years. It was during this time that Moses had one of the greatest privileges that anyone has ever known. God told Moses to go to the top of a mountain called Sinai. For forty days and nights Moses was there in the presence of God, talking with Him. When he returned, God's glow was upon his face and God's words were in his hands. Moses carried tablets of stone, and on the tablets were the ten commandments. God gave these commandments because He loved His people. The commandments showed them the best possible way anyone could ever live. It showed them a life of wholeness and goodness, a life of purity and kindness, and a life of holiness and love.

Based on Exodus 1-20

God has always worked through people to do His will. The people God uses are people of faith—people who listen to Him and follow what He says. The Bible is filled with the stories of those who had faith in God, and let God use them. Moses was that kind of person. The Bible uses the word "meekness" to describe Moses. Meekness does not mean weakness, it means that He was teachable and that his will was yielded to God.

It took Moses a long time to learn the importance of meekness. When he was younger, he tried to do God's will by listening to his own plans instead of God's. When Moses realized that his plans would not work, he became discouraged, and went off to a desert place to live. He grew old, and had given up any hope of God ever using him, but God had other ideas. When Moses least expected it, God showed up. God spoke to him out of a burning bush that wouldn't burn up. It was a sign that caused Moses to realize that God can reveal His glory through common things. Through that bush, God told Moses that He wanted to use him, and that He had a great work for him to do.

Moses looked at his own emptiness and wondered what God saw in him, and how God would be able to use him. But God looked beyond Moses' age, his weak speech, and his tired body. God looked at Moses' heart and found faith there. Moses was to learn that the only thing he needed in order to do God's will was God's presence. To assure Moses of this, God pointed him to the most lifeless, powerless thing Moses knew of, the rod that was in his hand. Moses understood that the rod was nothing, that it possessed nothing, and could do nothing—it was just a dead stick!

The rod became a symbol of God's presence, and a picture of Moses' total dependence upon God. When Moses stood before Pharaoh, the rod was there, being used to send the ten plagues on Egypt…when Israel stood before the Red Sea, the rod was stretched out as the waters parted…when the Jewish people thirsted in the desert, the rod smote the rock as water gushed forth….when enemies fought against God's people, Moses lifted his rod and the victory was won.

We are all ordinary people, but it is our faith in an extraordinary God that makes the difference in our lives. God is still looking for people today that He can work through to touch the lives of others. God does not look at our ability when He wants to use us. Instead, He looks at our hearts. He looks for hearts that will trust Him and obey Him, hearts that will be available to do His will.

God Uses Ordinary Things and Ordinary People

Personal Heritage Page

RECALLING GOD'S FAITHFULNESS IN MY LIFE
FOR MY CHILDREN AND GRANDCHILDREN TO ALWAYS REMEMBER.

How God used me to touch someone's life:

_____

_____

_____

_____

_____

_____

_____

Date: _____

_____

_____

_____

_____

_____

_____

Date: _____

Date:

Date:

"So the next generation would know them, even the children yet to be born, and they in turn would tell their children. Then they would put their trust in God and would not forget His deeds but would keep His commands."

PSALM 78:6-7

THE ARK OF THE COVENANT

God's presence and His Word

are never

separated

The Heritage of Scripture

" 'There, above the cover between the two cherubim that are over the ark of the Testimony, I will meet with you and give you all My commands for the Israelites.' "

EXODUS 25:22

"How can a young man keep his way pure? By living according to Your word."

PSALM 119:9

"I rejoice in following Your statutes as one rejoices in great riches. I meditate on Your precepts and consider Your ways. I delight in Your decrees; I will not neglect Your word."

PSALM 119:14-16

"I run in the path of Your commands, for You have set my heart free."

PSALM 119:32

"You are my portion, O Lord; I have promised to obey Your words. I have sought Your face with all my heart; be gracious to me according to Your promise."

PSALM 119:57-58

"I will bow down toward Your holy temple and will praise Your name for Your love and Your faithfulness, for You have exalted above all things Your name and Your Word."

PSALM 138:2

"The Word became flesh and made His dwelling among us. We have seen His glory, the glory of the One and Only, who came from the Father, full of grace and truth…."

JOHN 1:14

"For the word of the Lord is right and true; He is faithful in all He does."

PSALM 33:4

"Many peoples will come and say, 'Come, let us go up to the mountain of the Lord, to the house of the God of Jacob. He will teach us His ways, so that we may walk in His paths.' The law will go out from Zion, the word of the Lord from Jerusalem."

ISAIAH 2:3

When God first called Moses to meet Him at the top of Mount Sinai, he had to pass through a thick cloud. This cloud kept Moses' meeting with God out of the view of the people. While Moses was on Mount Sinai for forty days, the Hebrew people grew impatient. They believed Moses was gone too long and perhaps would never return. Instead of waiting on God to hear what He wanted to say to them, they decided to create their own god out of gold in the shape of a calf. It was a god that couldn't see or speak, so they felt safe in its presence, thinking that they could do anything they wanted. When they turned from God, they quickly turned to evil.

On the mountain, God was telling wonderful things to Moses. God told him about His love for His people, and His future plans for them. God gave instructions on how the people should live and worship. Most of all, God spoke about His presence with the people. In order for them to understand the meaning of His presence and its importance, God told Moses to build a special wooden chest that would be covered inside and out with gold.

The chest would be called the Ark of the Covenant. Moses was told that God's law, the Ten Commandments, was to be placed inside the Ark. On the outside of the Ark was to be a special place called the Mercy Seat. On each end of the Mercy Seat cherubim were to be positioned with their wings stretched out over the Mercy Seat. The Ark was to also have four rings attached to it, and two long poles placed through the rings. Everything on the outside of the Ark was also to be made of wood and covered with gold.

The Ark was God's way of telling His people that His Word and His presence could never be separated. As His Word was inside the Ark, so God's Word was also to be kept in the people's hearts. The Mercy Seat was the place where God's presence would dwell. As the poles where attached to the Ark so that it could be carried, so God's Word and His presence were to be carried with them always.

When Moses returned from the mountain and saw the sin of the people, he broke the stone tablets he carried. The people were severely judged for their sin and changed the way they were living. Moses was called back to the mountain by God and given the commandments once again. This time the people willingly listened to Moses. They gave an offering that allowed workers, who were gifted by God's Spirit, to build the Ark according to God's plan. When the Ark was completed, the law of God was placed inside, and the Ark went with the Jewish people throughout their journeys.

Based on Exodus 19-25

After God led Moses and the Jewish people out of Egypt, His plan was to lead them into the land of Canaan, the promised land that would be their home. Before they arrived, God guided them through the desert. His purpose was to test their hearts, so that they would trust Him and follow His words, even under very difficult circumstances. It was important for them to learn the lessons of trust and obedience, for the land that God was bringing them into had many enemies to conquer. God knew that the people would not be ready to enter the promised land and be victorious unless they followed Him and trusted Him completely. The people needed to walk in God's holiness so that they would not take part in the sins of their enemies…they needed to listen to God's truth, so that they would not believe the lies of their enemies…they needed to depend upon God's strength, so that they would not be overcome by the power of their enemies.

Time and time again in the desert, the people failed to listen to God or to trust Him completely. Their hearts were stubborn and bitter. Instead of trust, they were filled with fear…instead of hope, they were filled with despair…instead of peace, they were filled with anger. All through this time God was a loving Father to them. He cared for them in their need and disciplined them in their rebellion. He humbled them so that they would learn that God was the most important thing in their lives.

After their long, hard journey in the desert, the people arrived at the banks of the Jordan River. The time had come for them to enter the promised land. The people sent out spies to look the land over. When the spies returned, only two of them reported back with God's words—words of faith, promise, victory and hope. Instead, the people listened to the other spies, the one's whose words were filled with worry, anxiety, and unbelief.

As they listened to the wrong words, their hearts became terrified and they refused to enter the land. Instead of moving forward, they went back; instead of conquering, they were conquered. For forty years God was grieved with the people He had taken out of Egypt, but He never forsook them or left them alone. Because they did not listen to Him, they did not have His blessings on their lives. They continued to see God's works, but never learned His ways. They continued to live in defeat, when they could have seen God's conquering hand…they continued to sleep upon the sand, when they could have pitched their tents under the shade trees of Canaan…they continued to eat manna, when they could have feasted in the land of milk and honey.

After the death of Moses, a new leader and a new generation would enter the promised land. The leader was Joshua. Joshua knew that total victory would be his as he kept God's Word in his heart and on his lips, and obeyed Him completely.

God's Presence and His Word are Never Separated

Personal Heritage Page

RECALLING GOD'S FAITHFULNESS IN MY LIFE
FOR MY CHILDREN AND GRANDCHILDREN TO ALWAYS REMEMBER.

*Scriptures I have hidden in my heart
that have special meaning in my life:*

_____

_____

_____

_____

_____

_____

_____

_____

_____

_____

Date: _____

_____

_____

_____

_____

_____

_____

_____

_____

Date: _____

Date:

Date:

"So the next generation would know them, even the children yet to be born, and they in turn would tell their children. Then they would put their trust in God and would not forget His deeds but would keep His commands."

PSALM 78:6-7

THE STORY OF DAVID AND GOLIATH

God can do anything
but fail

The Heritage of Scripture

" 'The Lord who delivered me from the paw of the lion and the paw of the bear will deliver me from the hand of this Philistine.' David said to the Philistine, 'You come against me with sword and spear and javelin, but I come against you in the name of the Lord Almighty, the God of the armies of Israel, whom you have defied. This day the Lord will hand you over to me, and I'll strike you down and cut off your head…and the whole world will know that there is a God in Israel.' "

I SAMUEL 17:37, 45-46

" 'Is anything too hard for the Lord?…' "

GENESIS 18:14

" '…With God all things are possible.' "

MATTHEW 19:26

"Not one of all the Lord's good promises to the house of Israel failed; every one was fulfilled."

JOSHUA 21:45

"David also said to Solomon his son, 'Be strong and courageous, and do the work. Do not be afraid or discouraged, for the Lord God, my God, is with you. He will not fail you or forsake you until all the work for the service of the temple of the Lord is finished.' "

I CHRONICLES 28:20

" 'I will maintain my love to him forever, and My covenant with him will never fail.' "

PSALM 89:28

" 'As the rain and the snow come down from heaven, and do not return to it without watering the earth and making it bud and flourish, so that it yields seed for the sower and bread for the eater, so is My Word that goes out from My mouth: It will not return to Me empty, but will accomplish what I desire and achieve the purpose for which I sent it.' "

ISAIAH 55:10-11

"Your kingdom is an everlasting kingdom, and Your dominion endures through all generations. The Lord is faithful to all His promises and loving toward all He has made."

PSALM 145:13

" 'He is the Rock, His works are perfect, and all His ways are just. A faithful God who does no wrong, upright and just is He.' "

DEUTERONOMY 32:4

he nation of Israel's first king was named Saul. The people loved King Saul, but he was a king whose heart was not right toward God. Because of Saul's disobedience, God rejected him as king. In his place, God would choose a king who loved Him very much. One day, God sent his servant Samuel, to the house of Jesse. Samuel's job was to appoint one of Jesse's sons as Israel's new king. Samuel did not know which one of Jesse's eight sons God had chosen. When Samuel saw Jesse's first born son, Eliab, Samuel thought he had found the new king. But God told Samuel that Jesse's eldest son was not His choice. God reminded Samuel not to give importance to what a person looked like on the outside, but to give importance to what a person was like on the inside. God's choice for king was Jesse's youngest son, David. Many years would pass before God would place David over the nation of Israel as king. David still needed to grow in his faith, and in his understanding of God. During those years of preparation, Saul remained the king.

The nation of Israel had many enemies in the land in which they lived. One of their greatest enemies was the Philistines. They made war against king Saul and his army. The Philistines had a great warrior named Goliath. Goliath challenged anyone in Israel to a battle—winner take all. No one in Israel's army had the courage to fight Goliath. For forty days Goliath challenged them. Each time he did, Israel's fear of Goliath grew greater. It was at this time that Jesse sent his youngest son, David, to the place of battle. David was not sent as a soldier to fight, but as a servant to bring food to his older brothers. When David arrived at the scene and witnessed the challenge of Goliath, he took action. As David listened to Goliath's defiance, his opinion of Goliath decreased, as his faith in God increased. David knew that Goliath was no match for the living God.

David quickly found his way to Saul. David asked him for permission to face Goliath in battle. At first Saul refused, then he reconsidered, and finally he consented to David's request. Saul tried to put his armor on David, but David knew that what worked for Saul would not work for him. David set out to face Goliath without a shield, helmet, or sword. Dressed only in his shepherd's clothes, and armed only with his shepherd's sling and five smooth stones, David faced Goliath.

Goliath came at David with insult, David came at Goliath with authority…Goliath came at David in the might of his flesh, David came at Goliath in the power of God's Spirit…Goliath used fear, David used faith…Goliath roared out laughter, David slung out a stone…Goliath thought he'd carry off David's body, David carried off Goliath's head. God gave David a great victory. From this moment on, the hearts of the people began to turn away from Saul, and turn toward David, the shepherd boy who would one day be their king.

Based on I Samuel 16-17

When David was young, he was given the job of caring for his father's sheep. As a shepherd, David learned that God was like a shepherd—providing for and protecting His people in the same way that a shepherd cares for his sheep. As David leaned on his shepherd's staff for support, he knew that he could lean upon God's strength in all things. In the peaceful moments David spent on the hillsides with his flock, David rested in God's quiet presence. He often thought about the wonder of God's creation, the beauty of God's character, and the glory of God's ways. David's heart knew God's heart…his feet followed God's paths…his music sounded God's praise…his voice sang God's songs.

David knew that he didn't have to wait until he was older before he could have faith in God. He knew that he didn't have to be a mighty king before God could use him. He knew that he didn't have to be a soldier in Israel's army before he could have God's help in fighting his battles. One day, when David was with his flock, he discovered that a lion had attacked one of the sheep and had taken it away. David went after the lion, rescued the sheep from the lion's mouth, and killed the lion. On another occasion, a bear also took one of the sheep from the flock. David went after the bear, rescued the sheep, and killed the bear. David didn't do these brave things because he was big and strong, or because he had great and powerful weapons. He did them because He knew who God was, and what God could do. David trusted God to be his strength and to give him the victory.

It was very important for David to learn these lessons of faith as he watched over his sheep. God was preparing David for the time when he would watch over the people of Israel as their king. God was making David a king on the inside, before God made him a king on the outside. David learned to be gentle with people, and to be strong against God's enemies…to be patient when others misunderstood him, and to charge ahead when it was time to take action…to be humble when others had authority over him, and to be in command when he was given leadership.

David's faith in God prepared him for the future. If David didn't know God's voice, he could not have faced Goliath's threats…if he didn't know God's protection, he could not have faced Goliath's spear…if he didn't know God's strength, he could not have faced Goliath's might. David's faith stood strong because he knew that the God who delivered him from the lion and the bear would also deliver him from the hand of Goliath.

David stood before the giant, Goliath, and conquered him because David's heart knew that God could do anything—but fail.

God Can Do Anything But Fail

Personal Heritage Page

RECALLING GOD'S FAITHFULNESS IN MY LIFE
FOR MY CHILDREN AND GRANDCHILDREN TO ALWAYS REMEMBER.

Things that God has done for me in the past that help me trust Him for the future: _____

_____

_____

_____

_____

_____

_____

Date: _____

_____

_____

_____

_____

_____

_____

Date: _____

Date:

Date:

" So the next generation would know them, even the children yet to be born, and they in turn would tell their children. Then they would put their trust in God and would not forget His deeds but would keep His commands."

PSALM 78:6-7

THE STORY OF DANIEL

God
answers
Prayer

The Heritage of Scripture

"…At this, Daniel went in to the king and asked for time, so that he might interpret the dream for him. Then Daniel returned to his house and explained the matter to his friends…He urged them to plead for mercy from the God of heaven concerning this mystery, so that he and his friends might not be executed with the rest of the wise men of Babylon. During the night the mystery was revealed to Daniel in a vision. Then Daniel praised the God of heaven."

DANIEL 2:16-19

" 'Ask and it will be given to you; seek and you will find; knock and the door will be opened to you. For everyone who asks receives; he who seeks finds; and to him who knocks, the door will be opened.' "

MATTHEW 7:7-8

" 'I tell you the truth, anyone who has faith in Me will do what I have been doing. He will do even greater things than these, because I am going to the Father. And I will do whatever you ask in My name, so that the Son may bring glory to the Father.' "

JOHN 14:12-13

"This is the confidence we have in approaching God: that if we ask anything according to His will, He hears us. And if we know that He hears us—whatever we ask—we know that we have what we asked of Him."

I JOHN 5:14-15

" 'But when you pray, go into your room, close the door and pray to your Father, who is unseen. Then your Father, who sees what is done in secret, will reward you. And when you pray, do not keep on babbling like pagans, for they think they will be heard because of their many words. Do not be like them, for your Father knows what you need before you ask Him.' "

MATTHEW 6:6-8

"Then Jesus told His disciples a parable to show them that they should always pray and not give up."

LUKE 18:1

"…The prayer of a righteous man is powerful and effective."

JAMES 5:16

"I call to the Lord, who is worthy of praise, and I am saved from my enemies."

PSALM 18:3

Daniel was a young Jewish teenager when Nebuchadnezzar, the king of Babylon, attacked Jerusalem. Even though Daniel was obedient to God, the Jewish people were not. Because of this, God allowed Nebuchadnezzar to take the people captive and bring them to Babylon. When Daniel arrived, he soon discovered that the king wanted to change him. In place of his Jewish name, the king gave him a Babylonian name. The king also wanted to change Daniel's diet, education, and the way he lived. Daniel did not bend to the king's pressures, and refused to do anything that would displease God. Because Daniel did not give in and do what he was asked to do, God honored him, and gave him great favor. When Daniel was in the presence of the king, the king discovered that Daniel was a person of integrity and wisdom.

One night the king had a dream that troubled him. He didn't understand its meaning, and he called in the wise people of the land to explain his dream. Then he did something that had never been done before—he asked not only that his dream be explained, but he said, "First, I want you to tell me what my dream was about." No one in the king's service could do that. It was an impossible task. The wise people said, "Tell us what your dream was about, then we can tell you what it means." The king grew angry and demanded that he be given the dream and the explanation—if not, he would have all the wise men of Babylon put to death. When Daniel heard of the king's plan, Daniel didn't panic—he prayed. Daniel was confident that God knew both the dream and the interpretation. God answered Daniel's prayer. Daniel went before the king and told him his dream and its meaning. Daniel told the king that through his dream, God was revealing things that would happen in the future. The king was overcome with amazement. He praised the God of Daniel, and made Daniel a ruler in the land. In time, king Nebuchadnezzar died. His son, Belshazzar, became king. He was an evil man who mocked God. God judged him for his evil, and a foreign king, named Darius, conquered the land.

God continued to honor Daniel, and king Darius desired to place Daniel in charge of his entire kingdom. The people who served the king became jealous when they heard of the king's plans. They watched Daniel closely to see if they could find fault with him. They did this to take away his power. They could find no fault with him, so they decided to trap him. They discovered that Daniel openly prayed three times a day. With this knowledge they went to the king and told him to make a new law, stating that for thirty days the only one the people could pray to was the king. The king foolishly agreed, and signed a law that could not be changed or cancelled. Daniel would not obey the law. As punishment, he was thrown into a den of lions. The king was sorry for what he had done, but could not stop it. The next day the king's heart rejoiced when he discovered that God's angel had kept the lions' mouths shut and saved Daniel's life.

Based on Daniel 1-6

*W*hen Daniel lived in the land of Israel, he learned to know God, and discovered many things about His character and His ways. When the land of Israel was invaded, and Daniel was taken captive to Babylon, the people of that land were to learn many things about God too. In a way, Daniel was the best and the worst thing that ever happened to Babylon. It was the best for those who listened to the things that God was saying to them through Daniel; it was the worst for those who resisted Daniel and rebelled against God.

Daniel was taken to a nation with great military power, but weak moral strength…to a king who hungered after knowledge, but who did not seek after God…to a people who were religious, but who worshiped idols. Daniel's life was a light to those who lived in darkness…a pillar of strength to those whose lives were crumbling like sand…a voice of truth to those who spoke lies and deceit. To the king, Daniel pointed the way to the King of Kings. To the magicians, Daniel demonstrated the power and wisdom of the living God. To the idol worshippers, Daniel declared the glory of the God who answers prayer. The Babylonians had gods with eyes that could not see, and ears that could not hear—gods made with human hands that could not even perform human tasks. Daniel's God was the true God— the One who could do the impossible, because all things were possible for Him.

Daniel prayed because he knew that God answered prayer. Daniel knew that God's ears were open to hear his prayers, and that God's heart desired to bless him. He prayed to worship and to give thanks, because God was worthy. He prayed because He believed that God was in charge of all His creation, and that He also had the authority to make a person a king or remove him from power. He knew that God sees what people think is hidden…that God knows what people think is unknowable…and that God does what people think is undoable. When dreams needed to be known, Daniel prayed. When visions needed to be interpreted, Daniel prayed. When he was commanded to worship idols, Daniel prayed. When his life was being threatened, Daniel prayed. As Daniel bowed before God in humility, God raised him up to a place of great honor. As Daniel set his face to seek God, the light of God's glory shone upon him.

God used Daniel to speak His words to Kings, to those who worked for kings, and to those who served kings. To those who listened, God revealed great mysteries of His will. To those who resisted, God brought swift judgement. God humbled the proud, confused the wise, weakened the strong, destroyed the destroyers, and dethroned those who sat upon thrones. In all things God showed Himself good, declared Himself mighty, and revealed Himself as the One who is in control.

God Answers Prayer

Personal Heritage Page

RECALLING GOD'S FAITHFULNESS IN MY LIFE
FOR MY CHILDREN AND GRANDCHILDREN TO ALWAYS REMEMBER.

Prayers that God has answered:

_____

_____

_____

_____

_____

_____

_____

_____

Date: _____

_____

_____

_____

_____

_____

_____

_____

Date: _____

Date:

Date:

" So the next generation would know them, even the children yet to be born, and they in turn would tell their children. Then they would put their trust in God and would not forget His deeds but would keep His commands."

PSALM 78:6-7

THE STORY OF THE WISE MEN

Seeing Jesus

The Heritage of Scripture

"After they had heard the king, they went on their way, and the star they had seen in the east went ahead of them until it stopped over the place where the Child was. When they saw the star, they were overjoyed. On coming to the house, they saw the Child with His mother Mary, and they bowed down and worshiped Him…."

MATTHEW 2:9-11

"The Word became flesh and made His dwelling among us. We have seen His glory, the glory of the One and Only, who came from the Father, full of grace and truth."

JOHN 1:14

"Simeon took him in his arms and praised God, saying: 'Sovereign Lord, as You have promised, You now dismiss Your servant in peace. For my eyes have seen Your salvation, which You have prepared in the sight of all people, a light for revelation to the Gentiles and for glory to Your people Israel.' "

LUKE 2:28-32

"Now there were some Greeks among those who went up to worship at the Feast. They came to Philip, who was from Bethsaida in Galilee, with a request. 'Sir,' they said, 'we would like to see Jesus.' "

JOHN 12:20-21

"Let us fix our eyes on Jesus, the author and perfecter of our faith, who for the joy set before Him endured the cross, scorning its shame, and sat down at the right hand of the throne of God."

HEBREWS 12:2

"But we see Jesus, who was made a little lower than the angels, now crowned with glory and honor because He suffered death, so that by the grace of God He might taste death for everyone."

HEBREWS 2:9

"For the law was given through Moses; grace and truth came through Jesus Christ. No one has ever seen God, but God the One and Only, who is at the Father's side, has made Him known."

JOHN 1:17-18

"He is the image of the invisible God, the firstborn over all creation. For by Him all things were created: things in heaven and on earth, visible and invisible, whether thrones or powers or rulers or authorities; all things were created by Him and for Him. He is before all things, and in Him all things hold together."

COLOSSIANS 1:15-17

When Daniel was taken captive to Babylon, he brought a great spiritual influence to the people of the east. His godly wisdom influenced the wise men of that land, and his obedience to God influenced the rulers of the land. Daniel's life was a testimony to Scripture and a witness of God's faithfulness. One of the prophecies that Daniel was given spoke of God's future plans for the nations. It also spoke of the time when the Messiah, God's promised Son, would come. Some four hundred years later, this heritage, left by Daniel, gave the wise men of the East a reason to begin to look for a sign that would announce the new King's coming.

One day, as they searched the heavens, the sign appeared. It was a star—one that was different from any they had ever seen. When they saw it they understood that this star was God's birth announcement to them, declaring that the king of the Jews was born. The prophesy of Daniel had been fulfilled. Their faith prompted them to see the new king. They knew the way to Jerusalem, and traveled there because it was the Jewish city for royalty. The wise men assumed that once they arrived in the city, the Jewish people could give them directions to where the new king was staying. When they arrived in the city, instead of finding people filled with joy and celebration, they found only silence and ignorance. No one knew a thing about a newborn Jewish king.

Their inquiries stirred up the city, causing the Roman king, Herod, to speak with them. Herod did not consider the wise men's words good news, instead, he saw it as a threat to his kingdom. When the wise men left him, Herod wondered how the Jewish scribes and religious leaders could have missed the birth of their Jewish king, while Gentiles from a far off country knew of it.

When the wise men left Herod, they wondered where to go. Suddenly, the star that first appeared in the East, now appeared to them again. The star that was once used as a sign, was now being used by God as a guide. They were overjoyed. The star remained in the sky until it brought them to the exact house where the new king was staying. They didn't find the king in a beautiful palace, but in a common home. They didn't find him wearing royal robes, but wearing simple clothes. They didn't find him surrounded by loyal subjects, but supported by a humble, caring family. When they saw him their hearts were satisfied, their souls were peaceful, and their spirits were filled with admiration. They presented him with gifts that they carried from their homeland, and when they had completed their visit, they departed. They did not return home the same way they had come, because God warned them in a dream not to return to king Herod. The wise men returned home with greater gifts than they had left behind, for in their hearts they carried the treasures of the love of Jesus Christ.

Based on Matthew 2

The wise men saw what others failed to see, they heard what others failed to hear, and they traveled where others failed to go. Their eyes searched the heavens, and discovered the star that would direct them to a new King...their ears listened to God's Word, and believed the message that would bring them new hope…their feet followed God's leading, and found the One who would bring them new life. The wise men were seekers who became finders, and they became keepers. They searched for God with all their hearts and found Him. The meaningful things that they discovered on their journey, they were able to keep with them forever. They left their homes in faith, and returned home with great joy…they left their homes carrying earthly gifts, and returned home with heavenly treasures…they left their homes filled with wonder, and returned home with worship in their hearts.

The wise men lived in a land that was far away from the place where Jesus was born. They lived among people whose hearts were far away from the Gift that God wanted to bring them. But, the wise men were not in a place that was too far away for God to find them. When the wise men looked to God, their eyes were filled with light. The wise men saw far more than the new King's star that appeared in the heavens. The wise men saw that the star was the Star of Jacob, and that the new King was the promised Messiah of Israel. They saw that this was not the time for the King to conquer kingdoms, but the time for Him to conquer hearts…that this was not the time when He would sit on a royal throne, but that He would live in lowliness and walk in humility….that this was not the time for Him to wear a crown, but the time when he would die for the sins of all. Because of this, as they prepared themselves for their long journey, they carefully gathered the perfect gifts that they would place before him.

The wise men packed a gift of gold—a gift that would be used to meet the needs of the child and his family, and one that was fitting His royalty. They packed the gift of frankincense—a gift that was used in offering worship and adoration, and one that was fitting His deity. They packed the gift of myrrh—a gift that was used for burial, and one that was fitting His death.

The wise men saw God's promise in the Scriptures, His sign in the heavens, and His wisdom in a dream. But, the greatest thing their eyes beheld was Jesus' gentle face. As their physical eyes gazed upon Him, their spiritual eyes saw a beauty they had never known, a majesty they had never seen, and a wonder they had never imagined. The more they saw, the deeper they worshiped and the fuller their hearts became. When they saw Jesus, they gave Him more than earthly gifts—they gave Him their lives and their love.

Seeing Jesus

Personal Heritage Page

RECALLING GOD'S FAITHFULNESS IN MY LIFE
FOR MY CHILDREN AND GRANDCHILDREN TO ALWAYS REMEMBER.

Things that God's Word and God's Spirit have shown me about Jesus:

_____

_____

_____

_____

_____

_____

_____

_____

Date: _____

_____

_____

_____

_____

_____

_____

Date: _____

Date:

Date:

"So the next generation would know them, even the children yet to be born, and they in turn would tell their children. Then they would put their trust in God and would not forget His deeds but would keep His commands."

PSALM 78:6-7

THE STORY OF JOSEPH AND THE FLIGHT INTO EGYPT

Trusting God in

difficult times

The Heritage of Scripture

"…An angel of the Lord appeared to Joseph in a dream. 'Get up,' he said, 'take the Child and His mother and escape to Egypt. Stay there until I tell you, for Herod is going to search for the Child to kill Him.' So he got up, took the Child and His mother during the night and left for Egypt…."

MATTHEW 2:13-14

"God is our refuge and strength, an ever-present help in trouble."

PSALM 46:1

"…God has said, 'Never will I leave you; never will I forsake you.' So we say with confidence, 'The Lord is my helper; I will not be afraid. What can man do to me?' "

HEBREWS 13:5-6

"I was young and now I am old, yet I have never seen the righteous forsaken or their children begging bread."

PSALM 37:25

"The Lord is my shepherd, I shall not be in want. He makes me lie down in green pastures, He leads me beside quiet waters, He restores my soul. He guides me in paths of righteousness for His name's sake. Even though I walk through the valley of the shadow of death, I will fear no evil, for You are with me; Your rod and Your staff, they comfort me. You prepare a table before me in the presence of my enemies. You anoint my head with oil; my cup overflows. Surely goodness and love will follow me all the days of my life, and I will dwell in the house of the Lord forever."

PSALM 23:1-6

"When I am afraid, I will trust in you."

PSALM 56:3

"I lift up my eyes to the hills—where does my help come from? My help comes from the Lord, the Maker of heaven and earth. He will not let your foot slip—He who watches over you will not slumber; indeed, He who watches over Israel will neither slumber nor sleep. The Lord watches over you—the Lord is your shade at your right hand; the sun will not harm you by day, nor the moon by night. The Lord will keep you from all harm—He will watch over your life; the Lord will watch over your coming and going both now and forevermore."

PSALM 121:1-8

oseph was a good and righteous man, who lived in a city called Nazareth. His family line went back to king David. He is a great example of a humble man, that God used in quiet ways, to do great things. When God spoke to Joseph in a dream and told him to take Mary as his wife, he willingly accepted the great responsibility that would be his. Joseph knew that the Child she carried was conceived by the Holy Spirit, and that the Child was the promised Saviour. When a long and difficult trip had to be taken before the birth of Mary's baby, Joseph lovingly protected her and provided for her every need on their journey. When the Child was about to be born, Joseph sought out a place in the busy city of Bethlehem where Mary could have privacy and care. When the time came for Jesus to be brought to the temple in Jerusalem, Joseph faithfully followed all that the law required.

After this, a time came when Joseph's faith in God would be tested in a new way. The journey of the wise men from the East had finally brought them to the house where Joseph, Mary, and the Child, Jesus, lived. Their visit brought great encouragement to Joseph. The gifts that they gave the Child were graciously and gratefully received. During the wise men's visit, Joseph was not aware of the jealousy that raged within Herod, and his evil plan to find and kill the young Child. When the visitors from the East left, Joseph thought about the meaning of all the things they had said and done.

That night, as Joseph slept, an angel of God appeared to him. The angel was not a stranger to Joseph, for the angel had appeared to him at other times. The angel told Joseph of Herod's evil plan, and of the great danger the Child faced. Joseph was instructed by the angel to take Mary and the Child, and to leave immediately for the land of Egypt. Whenever God spoke to Joseph, Joseph listened. He did not waste time trying to reason with the angel, or trying to figure out God's plan. Joseph's obedience was immediate. In the dark of night, Joseph quickly gathered the things his family would need for their journey, and fled to the land of Egypt.

Once again Joseph was dependent upon God. He left the land he knew and loved, to go to a strange country with a different language and different ways. Despite the new difficulties that Joseph would face when he arrived in Egypt, he was certain that the safest place for his family was in the place that God asked them to be. Joseph was willing to patiently remain in Egypt until the time that God told him it was safe to return to his homeland. When Joseph returned home, he settled once again with his family in the city of Nazareth. He went to work there and provided for the needs of his family—and there Jesus grew in favor with God and man, and learned to be a carpenter from the hands of Joseph.

Based on Matthew 2

Throughout the Scriptures, God promises His peace, presence, power, provision, and protection. Joseph knew those promises and trusted God completely. Joseph also knew from Scripture that God had never promised a life free of sorrow, pain, testing, hardship, sacrifice, or suffering. Joseph understood that those who received God's promises often experienced great difficulties that tested their faith and trust in the faithfulness of God. But, Joseph also knew that God always used those times for good, to glorify His name, and to accomplish His special purposes. Joseph's faith in God assured him that he would never walk through a difficult time without God's eye upon him, His presence with him, His hand over him, and His love surrounding him.

From the first moment that Joseph heard God speak to him, Joseph's heart willingly listened, humbly received, and gladly obeyed. As a young man, Joseph kept himself pure and did what was right. As an engaged man, Joseph treated his future bride, Mary, with honor and respect. As a husband, he took the place of a loving leader and a caring servant.

As a family man, he accepted his calling, faced responsibility, did his duty, and provided protection. In all things, he made choices that were the best, even though they were not always easy. He made decisions that were right, even though they were not always popular. Joseph lived for only one thing— the approval of God.

Joseph totally depended on God for all the things that God asked Him to do. He depended on God to keep Mary well and safe on their long journey to Bethlehem when the census was being taken. He depended on God for a place where Mary could deliver her Child when there was no room for them in the inn. He depended on God for his sudden journey into Egypt when the life of the young Child, Jesus, was in danger. And he depended on God to tell him when the time would be safe for him to return from Egypt to his homeland.

In his dependence, Joseph's faith in God grew stronger and his love for God grew deeper. Joseph wanted what God wanted for his life. He was never sorry that he'd followed God's plan for his life, for he knew that God did not make any mistakes. In the times of testing, Joseph saw the wisdom of God's ways…in the times of need, Joseph saw that God always provided…in the times of darkness, Joseph saw the light of God's love. To follow God completely Joseph had to be willing to give up the comforts of his home, the companionship of his friends, the closeness of his family, the security of his work, and the support of his community. In return, Joseph gained the smile of God upon Him, the blessings of God over him, and the peace of God within him. Joseph's hands held the Son of God, Joseph's eyes watched Him grow, and Joseph's heart became filled with the wonders of God's amazing love.

Trusting God in Difficult Times

Personal Heritage Page

RECALLING GOD'S FAITHFULNESS IN MY LIFE
FOR MY CHILDREN AND GRANDCHILDREN TO ALWAYS REMEMBER.

Difficult times that God has brought me through:

_____

_____

_____

_____

_____

_____

_____

Date: _____

_____

_____

_____

_____

_____

_____

Date: _____

Date:

Date:

"So the next generation would know them, even the children yet to be born, and they in turn would tell their children. Then they would put their trust in God and would not forget His deeds but would keep His commands."

PSALM 78:6-7

God's ways are the best ways to live

The Heritage of Scripture

" 'Blessed are the poor in spirit, for theirs is the kingdom of heaven.
Blessed are those who mourn, for they will be comforted.
Blessed are the meek, for they will inherit the earth.
Blessed are those who hunger and thirst for righteousness, for they will be filled.
Blessed are the merciful, for they will be shown mercy.
Blessed are the pure in heart, for they will see God.
Blessed are the peacemakers, for they will be called sons of God.
Blessed are those who are persecuted because of righteousness, for theirs is the kingdom of heaven.' "

MATTHEW 5:3-10

" 'For My thoughts are not your thoughts, neither are your ways My ways,' declares the Lord. 'As the heavens are higher than the earth, so are My ways higher than your ways and My thoughts than your thoughts.' "

ISAIAH 55:8-9

"Trust in the Lord with all your heart and lean not on your own understanding; in all your ways acknowledge Him, and He will make your paths straight."

PROVERBS 3:5-6

"The law of the Lord is perfect, reviving the soul.
The statutes of the Lord are trustworthy, making wise the simple.
The precepts of the Lord are right, giving joy to the heart.
The commands of the Lord are radiant, giving light to the eyes.
The fear of the Lord is pure, enduring forever.
The ordinances of the Lord are sure and altogether righteous.
They are more precious than gold, than much pure gold;
they are sweeter than honey, than honey from the comb.
By them is Your servant warned; in keeping them there is great reward."

PSALM 19:7-11

"The thief comes only to steal and kill and destroy; I have come that they may have life, and have it to the full."

JOHN 10:10

"How lovely is Your dwelling place, O Lord Almighty! My soul yearns, even faints, for the courts of the Lord; my heart and my flesh cry out for the living God…Better is one day in Your courts than a thousand elsewhere; no good thing does He withhold from those whose walk is blameless."

PSALM 84:1-2, 10, 11

Everything about Jesus was different. No one would ever be born in the way He was born, no one would ever live in the way He lived, no one would ever speak in the way He spoke, no one could ever suffer in the way He suffered, and no one could ever die for the reason He died. Through His words, people heard what God was like; through His life, people saw what God was like.

Jesus grew up in the city of Nazareth. He lived a very quiet life, was obedient to Joseph and Mary, and learned the work of a carpenter. As He grew, His life pleased those who knew Him. When He reached the age of thirty, it was time for Him to begin His public ministry. He spent three years traveling throughout the land of Israel, doing good and proclaiming the Kingdom of God. Jesus was more than a good man, a prophet, or a teacher—He was God in human form.

At the start of His ministry, He chose twelve men to follow Him and be His disciples. As Jesus traveled, He did great works and mighty miracles. He healed people who were sick, gave sight to the blind, opened the ears of the deaf, made the lame to walk, and delivered those who were bound by Satan. All of these wonderful works of God caused Jesus' fame and popularity to grow. It seemed that everyone wanted to be where Jesus was so that they could see Him do wonders. On one occasion, when many people were following Him, Jesus went up a nearby mountain to teach them. His words would open their understanding to what the kingdom of God was all about—a kingdom that would come when they opened their hearts to Him, and let Him live His life inside them.

One of the important things He spoke about was the attitudes of the heart, attitudes that would bring inward blessings—blessings of joy and true satisfaction. Each right attitude revealed a proper response to sin. To those who were defeated by sin, He spoke words of hope; to those who were sorry for their sin, He spoke words of forgiveness; to those who were humbled by their sin, He spoke words of comfort; to those who wanted to be free of their sin, He spoke words of pardon; to those who had been hurt by the sins of others, He spoke words of mercy; to those who wanted to see beyond their sin, He spoke words of truth; to those who were troubled by sin, He spoke words of peace; for those who were treated wrongly because they no longer wanted to sin, He spoke words of acceptance and approval.

Jesus spoke about many other things that day. When He finished, the people were amazed. They had heard about how much their Father in Heaven loved them and cared for them, and how they could live a life that truly pleased God. That day every hungry heart went home full.

Based on Matthew 5-7

*M*ost people try to live their lives according to their own plans, and according to their own ideas. They try to get all they can, do all they can, and be all they can. They think that their way is the best way to live, and will bring them happiness. When Jesus taught, He told people that their ways were not God's ways, and that their thoughts were not God's thoughts. Jesus' words were arrows pointing people to the way of true joy. His teaching was not to make people feel better about the way they lived, but to have them change the way they lived. Jesus spoke with authority. He didn't hope His words could change people's lives, He knew they would. He didn't tell people what they wanted to hear, but what they needed to hear.

Jesus' words came from the heart of God, not from the mind of man. Wherever Jesus went, people's ears heard things that no teacher had ever said before…their eyes saw things that no person had ever seen before…their hearts were touched in ways that they had never felt before. To those who received what Jesus said, His words were like bread that they could feed upon, like light that they could gaze upon, and like rocks that they could stand upon. His words were seeds bringing new life, and signposts pointing to a new direction. His words were like sunshine, bringing warmth…like medicine, bringing healing…like water, bringing refreshment…like soap, bringing cleansing…and like food, bringing nourishment.

When Jesus spoke, people saw the true condition of their own hearts—His words revealed God's fullness, and showed people their emptiness…they revealed God's love, and showed people their selfishness…they revealed God's righteousness, and showed people their sinfulness. Jesus' words had power and brought conviction. His words made the rebellious angry, the doubters uncomfortable, the indifferent uneasy, and the self-confident unsure. His words declared that there was a different way, a higher way, a wiser way, and a better way to live.

Jesus' words were filled with compassion and love. His words spoke of a love that could only be found in God. Through His words, God was reaching out His arms to draw people close to His heart. He was embracing them with words of kindness, to bring them comfort…with words of goodness, to bring them encouragement…with words of mercy, to bring them hope. Jesus' words were eternal words that were filled with everlasting meaning, to bring never-ending life.

Jesus' words were words of promise. They were promises that people could depend upon, and that their faith could lean upon. His words were good news to the hearts that believed in Him, because His words would lead them into all the ways that were the very, very best.

God's Ways are the Best Ways to Live

Personal Heritage Page

RECALLING GOD'S FAITHFULNESS IN MY LIFE
FOR MY CHILDREN AND GRANDCHILDREN TO ALWAYS REMEMBER.

How I have learned that God's ways are the best ways to live:

Date:

Date:

Date:

Date:

"So the next generation would know them, even the children yet to be born, and they in turn would tell their children. Then they would put their trust in God and would not forget His deeds but would keep His commands."

PSALM 78:6-7

THE STORY OF JOHN THE BAPTIST

Saying "yes"
to God

The Heritage of Scripture

"A voice of one calling: 'In the desert prepare the way for the Lord; make straight in the wilderness a highway for our God. Every valley shall be raised up, every mountain and hill made low; the rough ground shall become level, the rugged places a plain. And the glory of the Lord will be revealed, and all mankind together will see it. For the mouth of the Lord has spoken.' "

ISAIAH 40:3-5

"So Eli told Samuel, 'Go and lie down, and if he calls you, say, "Speak, Lord, for your servant is listening."' So Samuel went and lay down in his place. The Lord came and stood there, calling as at the other times, 'Samuel! Samuel!' Then Samuel said, 'Speak, for your servant is listening.' "

I SAMUEL 3:9-10

" 'Hear, O Israel, and be careful to obey so that it may go well with you and that you may increase greatly in a land flowing with milk and honey, just as the Lord, the God of your fathers, promised you.' "

DEUTERONOMY 6:3

" 'But be very careful to keep the commandment and the law that Moses the servant of the Lord gave you: to love the Lord your God, to walk in all His ways, to obey His commands, to hold fast to Him and to serve Him with all your heart and all your soul.' "

JOSHUA 22:5

" 'Does the Lord delight in burnt offerings and sacrifices as much as in obeying the voice of the Lord? To obey is better than sacrifice….' "

I SAMUEL 15:22

"This is love for God: to obey His commands. And His commands are not burdensome."

I JOHN 5:3

"The people all responded together, 'We will do everything the Lord has said.' So Moses brought their answer back to the Lord."

EXODUS 19:8

"Therefore, I urge you, brothers, in view of God's mercy, to offer your bodies as living sacrifices, holy and pleasing to God—this is your spiritual act of worship. Do not conform any longer to the pattern of this world, but be transformed by the renewing of your mind. Then you will be able to test and approve what God's will is—His good, pleasing and perfect will."

ROMANS 12:1-2

*J*ohn was a miracle baby. His father was old and his mother was past the age of child-bearing. John's father, Zacharias, thought the idea of his wife expecting a child was so impossible that he doubted God's plan when the angel Gabriel told him of it. John's mother was named Elizabeth. She was the older cousin of Mary. Elizabeth gave birth to John six months before her cousin, Mary, gave birth to Jesus.

John's father, Zacharias, was a priest in the temple at Jerusalem. When the angel Gabriel first appeared to him, Zacharias was given important information about God's plan for the child. The angel told Zacharias what to name the child, how God was going to use the child, and how the child was to be raised. Zacharias knew from the start, that his son, John, did not belong to him, but to God. Both Zacharias and Elizabeth said "Yes" to God's plan, and it was an honor for them to be used of God in this way.

As John grew into manhood, he was separated from the ways of the world so that he could follow the ways of God. John's importance grew smaller in the eyes of people, but greater in the eyes of God. John emptied himself of pride, and was filled with God's Spirit…he lived alone in the desert, and enjoyed fellowship with God…he lived without wealth or possessions, but had the riches of God's kingdom in his heart. Shortly after his thirtieth birthday, God told John that the time for his public ministry had come. John was ready, and he set out to make the hearts of others ready for the coming of the Lord.

John's ministry would only last a few months. Even though the time of his ministry was short, there was nothing about John's life that was wasted. The important thing for John was not how long he ministered, but how faithful he was to what God called him to do. John not only said "Yes" to God's call on his life, but he said it gladly. John spent his time by the Jordan River, for it was there that he baptized those who confessed and repented of their sins. John told those who came to him that he was not the Messiah, but that the Messiah would soon appear. Six months after John began to preach, Jesus stepped into the Jordan River, and walked up to John. When John saw Him, he knew that his time of ministry was ending, and that Jesus' ministry was beginning.

John spoke the truth even though everyone did not want to listen to the truth. When John criticized the Roman ruler, Herod, about his evil ways, Herod placed John in prison. While John remained in prison, Herod made a foolish promise and agreed to have John put to death. Before the night was over, John's life ended, but the change he had made on the Roman Empire, on the nation of Israel, on the religious leaders of the land, and on the lives of the Jewish people would never be forgotten.

Based on Luke 1-3

Through the centuries there were many prophets that God used to speak His words and His will to the people. Their most important message foretold the coming of the Messiah to Israel. Isaiah, Jeremiah, and Ezekiel were some of the great prophets that God used to declare His message, but John was the greatest prophet of all. John was not greater because he was better than the other prophets, he was greater because of the special opportunity he was given by God. The other prophets could say that the Messiah would come, but John could say that the Messiah had come; the other prophets could point to the way of the Lord, but John prepared the way of the Lord; the other prophets longed to see the day of the Lord's coming, but John saw the Lord face to face.

God had a plan for John, and John followed that plan. God gave instructions to John, and he obeyed those instructions. God had set a time for John to be used, and he waited for that time. God had a message that He wanted John to preach, and John preached that message. John's heart was given to God, and his life was set apart for God. John had a single purpose—to prepare other people's hearts to receive the Messiah, Jesus Christ. He prepared them by warning them, by instructing them, by guiding them, and by baptizing them. John turned the spotlight off of himself and on to Jesus. John's only desire was that people would see less of him, and more of Jesus.

The more that people listened to John's words, the more they learned about Jesus. John told them that the Kingdom of God was coming, and that Jesus was the King of that Kingdom. He told them to turn from their sins, and to turn to the Lamb of God who would take their sins away. He told them that Jesus came from heaven, that He would return to heaven, and that He would take all who believed in Him to heaven. He told them about Jesus' greatness and His glory, about His majesty and His authority, about His purity and mercy. The more people listened to John, the more the excitement of seeing Jesus grew within them.

John was a clear signpost to those who didn't know which way to go, and a true voice to those who didn't know who to listen to. He prayed, he preached, he prophesied, he pointed, he proclaimed, and he prepared the way of the Lord. All those who listened to John had hearts that were right and ready because John's message changed the way people lived—those who had more than they needed gave to those who were without, those who had authority over others treated them with kindness, those who were in business treated their customers fairly, those who were in government treated people with respect, and those who received wages were happy with what they were paid. John's life was short, but his impact was everlasting. John gave up every natural comfort and pleasure in this world, so that others could receive heaven's priceless gift.

Saying "Yes" to God

Personal Heritage Page

RECALLING GOD'S FAITHFULNESS IN MY LIFE
FOR MY CHILDREN AND GRANDCHILDREN TO ALWAYS REMEMBER.

*Times when I've said
"Yes" to God and "No" to other things:* _____

_____

_____

_____

_____

_____

_____

_____

_____

Date: _____

_____

_____

_____

_____

_____

_____

_____

Date: _____

_____

_____

_____

_____

_____

_____

_____

_____

_____ *Date:* _____

_____

_____

_____

_____

_____

_____

_____

_____

_____ *Date:* _____

"So the next generation would know them, even the children yet to be born, and they in turn would tell their children. Then they would put their trust in God and would not forget His deeds but would keep His commands."

PSALM 78:6-7

THE HOLY SPIRIT

God's presence

THE HOLY SPIRIT

The Heritage of Scripture

"When all the people were being baptized, Jesus was baptized too. And as He was praying, heaven was opened and the Holy Spirit descended on Him in bodily form like a dove. And a voice came from heaven: 'You are my Son, whom I love; with You I am well pleased.' "

LUKE 3:21-22

" 'If you love Me, you will obey what I command. And I will ask the Father, and He will give you another Counselor to be with you forever—the Spirit of truth. The world cannot accept Him, because it neither sees Him nor knows Him. But you know Him, for He lives with you and will be in you. I will not leave you as orphans; I will come to you. But the Counselor, the Holy Spirit, whom the Father will send in My name, will teach you all things and will remind you of everything I have said to you.' "

JOHN 14:15-18, 26

"Do not cast me from your presence or take your Holy Spirit from me."

PSALM 51:11

" 'I baptize you with water for repentance. But after me will come one who is more powerful than I, whose sandals I am not fit to carry. He will baptize you with the Holy Spirit and with fire.' "

MATTHEW 3:11

" 'But you will receive power when the Holy Spirit comes on you; and you will be My witnesses in Jerusalem, and in all Judea and Samaria, and to the ends of the earth.' "

ACTS 1:8

"And the disciples were filled with joy and with the Holy Spirit."

ACTS 13:52

"And hope does not disappoint us, because God has poured out His love into our hearts by the Holy Spirit, whom He has given us."

ROMANS 5:5

"May the God of hope fill you with all joy and peace as you trust in Him, so that you may overflow with hope by the power of the Holy Spirit."

ROMANS 15:13

"For the kingdom of God is not a matter of eating and drinking, but of righteousness, peace and joy in the Holy Spirit."

ROMANS 14:17

"Do you not know that your body is a temple of the Holy Spirit, who is in you, whom you have received from God? You are not your own."

I CORINTHIANS 6:19

The presence and work of the Holy Spirit is found all through the Bible. In the beginning, when the earth and every living thing on it was made, the Holy Spirit was there doing His creative work. Whenever God called someone to do His will, the Holy Spirit was present with that person—giving the power, the wisdom, the guidance, and the ability to do God's will. The Holy Spirit was in the skills of those who built the temple, the creativity of those who made its furnishings, and the artistry of those who made the priestly garments. The Holy Spirit gave strategy to military leaders, courage to warriors, and wisdom to rulers. He was in the voice of the prophets, in the hands of the people who wrote the Bible, and in the counsel of the judges who ruled Israel. The Holy Spirit was in the aim of David's sling, the strength of Samson's arms, the shine of Moses' face, the interpretation of Daniel's dream, the sound of Joshua's trumpets, and the courage of Gideon's army. The Holy Spirit was the still small voice that spoke to Elijah, and the mighty rushing wind that filled the disciples on the day of Pentecost.

When Mary was told by the angel Gabriel that she would conceive and give birth to a Child, and that this Child was the Son of God, Mary wondered how this could be. The angel explained that the Holy Spirit would come upon her and perform this miracle. After this happened, Mary traveled to visit her cousin Elizabeth. When Mary entered Elizabeth's house and greeted her, the unborn baby, John, jumped for joy inside Elizabeth, and he was filled with the Holy Spirit. Later, when John was born, the Holy Spirit gave John's father a great prophecy about the work that John would do.

The most important work that the Holy Spirit would do was in the life and ministry of Jesus Christ. Jesus' earthly life began by the Holy Spirit. The Holy Spirit was with Jesus and in Jesus as He grew into manhood. When the time came for Jesus to begin the work He was sent to do, the Holy Spirit would be involved in Jesus' life in a new way. As Jesus came up out of the waters of baptism in the Jordan River, heaven opened and the Holy Spirit came upon Jesus like a dove landing gently upon Him. At the same time, God's voice spoke from heaven saying, "This is my Son, whom I love; with Him I am well pleased." The coming of the Holy Spirit like a dove was God's sign of approval upon Jesus' life.

The Holy Spirit had come upon Jesus to give Him power for all the things He would do and face during the next three years. Jesus would need the Holy Spirit to do signs and wonders…to heal hearts and bodies, and to make people whole…to resist Satan and cast out demons…to speak with authority and power…to face betrayal and endure suffering…to pray in the garden and be given over to his enemies…to be falsely accused and to die upon the cross…to suffer for sin and to be raised from the dead.

Based on Matthew 3 and Luke 1-2

The Holy Spirit is not an "it", a force, a thing, or an influence—the Holy Spirit is a person. He is part of the Godhead. In His nature, and character, He is Divine. The Holy Spirit is eternal—He has always been and always will be. He is all-powerful, is everywhere and knows all things. The Holy Spirit is God's presence with us today. Throughout the Scriptures we are given many pictures of the Holy Spirit. These pictures help us understand more about who the Holy Spirit is, and what He does. The Holy Spirit is like wind, moving in ways that we cannot see or understand; He is like water flowing out from God's throne to bring refreshing; He is like medicine pouring out God's healing touch; He is like fire cleansing the heart and making it pure; He is like a dove gently bringing the presence of God.

When Jesus went back to heaven after His resurrection from the dead, He sent the Holy Spirit to be with us. Jesus called the Holy Spirit "The Comforter." The Holy Spirit was sent to be with us and in us. He is the One who brings God's love, peace, and joy to our hearts, and God's power to our lives. The Holy Spirit is a comforter because He helps us to know that God is with us. The Holy Spirit is a counselor because He helps us understand all the things that Jesus taught us and all the things that Jesus did for us. The Holy Spirit is the One who brings new life to us, changing us on the inside. He is the One who helps us to know God's will, gives us the desire to do God's will, and brings us the power to live God's will.

In many ways the Holy Spirit is like a best friend. He encourages us when we get discouraged, He faithfully prays for us, and He supports us when we stand for what is right. He always tells us the truth, and He is always there to help us. He enjoys being with us and listens to us, He speaks to us with kindness and understanding, and He helps us grow strong in the Lord. He shares God's thoughts with us, He cares for us, and lovingly responds to our needs. The Holy Spirit is someone we can always turn to and lean upon for strength.

The Holy Spirit is the light that helps us to see Jesus…He is the guide that helps us to walk with Jesus…He is the teacher that helps us to know Jesus. He helps us speak to Jesus in prayer, and helps us share Jesus with others. The Holy Spirit will always lead us into everything that is good…He will always encourage us to reach for God's highest…He will always point us to everything that is best. Everything the Holy Spirit does is done in love, and with the purpose of glorifying God. He will never lead us away from God, or lead us into evil. He is pure and holy, and will never make us feel good about sin. The Holy Spirit gives us a purpose for life and a reason for living. He is our daily hope, our lasting peace, and our unending joy.

God's Presence

Personal Heritage Page

RECALLING GOD'S FAITHFULNESS IN MY LIFE
FOR MY CHILDREN AND GRANDCHILDREN TO ALWAYS REMEMBER.

What the presence of God in my life means to me: _____

_____

_____

_____

_____

_____

_____

Date:

_____

_____

_____

_____

_____

Date:

Date:

Date:

"So the next generation would know them, even the children yet to be born, and they in turn would tell their children. Then they would put their trust in God and would not forget His deeds but would keep His commands."

PSALM 78:6-7

THE STORY OF PAUL

God
changes
lives

The Heritage of Scripture

" 'Who are you, Lord?' Saul asked. 'I am Jesus, whom you are persecuting,' He replied. 'Now get up and go into the city, and you will be told what you must do.' "

ACTS 9:5-6

"I eagerly expect and hope that I will in no way be ashamed, but will have sufficient courage so that now as always Christ will be exalted in my body, whether by life or by death. For to me, to live is Christ and to die is gain."

PHILIPPIANS 1:20-21

"Your attitude should be the same as that of Christ Jesus."

PHILIPPIANS 2:5

"Do everything without complaining or arguing, so that you may become blameless and pure, children of God without fault in a crooked and depraved generation, in which you shine like stars in the universe."

PHILIPPIANS 2:14-15

"But whatever was to my profit I now consider loss for the sake of Christ. What is more, I consider everything a loss compared to the surpassing greatness of knowing Christ Jesus my Lord, for whose sake I have lost all things. I consider them rubbish, that I may gain Christ."

PHILIPPIANS 3:7-8

"Since, then, you have been raised with Christ, set your hearts on things above, where Christ is seated at the right hand of God. Set your minds on things above, not on earthly things. For you died, and your life is now hidden with Christ in God. When Christ, who is your life, appears, then you also will appear with Him in glory."

COLOSSIANS 3:1-4

"Therefore, if anyone is in Christ, he is a new creation; the old has gone, the new has come!"

II CORINTHIANS 5:17

"Whoever claims to live in Him must walk as Jesus did."

I JOHN 2:6

"Not that I have already obtained all this, or have already been made perfect, but I press on to take hold of that for which Christ Jesus took hold of me."

PHILIPPIANS 3:12

A t the day of Pentecost, the Holy Spirit came with power upon a small group of Jewish believers. After this, these believers began to tell others about all the things that Jesus said and did. They were His witnesses. As a result, thousands of Jews were coming to believe in Jesus as their Savior and Lord. Some of the Jewish religious leaders, who did not believe in Jesus, grew angry with those who said that Jesus was the way, the truth, and the life. These leaders began to speak against Jesus' followers and soon began to persecute them. One of these leaders was named Saul.

Saul was a Jew who had been strictly raised according to Jewish laws and customs. He was from the tribe of Benjamin and was trained to be a Pharisee—someone who strictly followed the laws of Moses, and thought he was better than others because of it. He grew up in Jerusalem and was taught by one of the leading Jewish teachers. Saul was very dedicated and sincere, but he was also wrong in his understanding of who Jesus was. In his dedication, Saul set out to stop those who were preaching and teaching the Gospel of Jesus Christ.

During this time, a group of Jewish leaders angrily listened to a man named Stephen speak about Jesus. When Stephen claimed to see Jesus standing in heaven, the group became so enraged that they captured him and stoned him to death. Saul was a witness to all of this, and willingly agreed to his death. After this, Saul worked even harder to stop the believers in Jesus. One day, he received special permission to travel to a city called Damascus and arrest or murder any Jewish person who believed.

As Saul prepared to go inside the city of Damascus, he was not prepared for what would happen to him just outside the city. There suddenly appeared a great light from heaven. The light was the presence of God, and it was so awesome that Saul fell to the ground. The light blinded his eyes, but opened his ears. Saul heard a voice and he immediately discovered that the One who was speaking to him was Jesus. At that very moment Saul changed his mind about who Jesus was, and Jesus changed Saul's life. The change was so great that later he would be called Paul instead of Saul.

When Saul was taken to Damascus, he entered the city as a willing follower of Jesus Christ, instead of a bitter enemy. This proud man was now a humble servant. While he was in the city, he learned of the plan that God had for his life. What Saul once thought to be unthinkable, was now something he found desirable—God was going to send him to proclaim Jesus not only to the Jews, but also to the Gentiles. For the rest of his life, Saul, who was now Paul, helped to turn the world upside down by turning people's lives right side up through faith in Jesus Christ.

Based on Acts 7-9

God never changes, but God changes lives. Paul was a man who experienced God's change. He changed from his old way of life to a new way of life. God changed Paul from living selfishly to living for Him…from a life of law to a life of grace…from a life of rules to a life of relationship. Paul's change caused him to love the things he once hated and to hate the things he once loved. His heart changed from being hard and stubborn to being tender and obedient. His will changed from making his own plans to following God's plans. His mind changed from thinking his own thoughts to thinking God's thoughts.

Paul was changed from darkness to light, from error to truth, from anger to gentleness, from sadness to joy, from restlessness to peace, and from unbelief to faith. Paul's change caused him to love those he had rejected, support those he tried to destroy, pray for those he had persecuted, reach out to those he had pushed away, and become a friend to those he had considered enemies. Paul became a new man with a new purpose for living. He had new goals, new desires, and new hope. He saw new things with his eyes, he heard new things with his ears, and he walked in new paths with his feet. He worked in new ways with his hands, he gave in new ways with his money, and he served in new ways with his strength. Paul now felt in new ways with his soul, he spoke in new ways with his words, he sang in new ways with his voice, and he worshiped in new ways with his heart.

When God changed Paul, the deepest things inside Paul changed—his desire was only to know Christ, his motivation was only to please Christ, his affection was only to love Christ, his passion was only to live for Christ, his goal was only to glorify Christ. God used the changes in Paul to bring changes to the world. God used Paul's pen to write God's word…God used Paul's preaching to bring many people into His Kingdom…God used Paul's teaching to help instruct and encourage God's church.

Paul became a true leader of men and a faithful servant of God. He lived with his conscience clear and his destiny certain. He counted everything he had as nothing because Christ was everything to him. In his weakness, Paul found God to be his strength. In his hardships, Paul found God to be his comfort. In Paul's travels, God was his companion…in his trials, God was his protector…in his needs, God was his provider. Paul was the Devil's enemy and God's friend. Paul faced hard times with endurance…times in prison with praise…times of temptation with purity…times of rejection with forgiveness…times of cruelty with kindness…times of need with contentment. He fought against sin with weapons of righteousness and marched against lies with the banner of truth.

God Changes Lives

Personal Heritage Page

RECALLING GOD'S FAITHFULNESS IN MY LIFE
FOR MY CHILDREN AND GRANDCHILDREN TO ALWAYS REMEMBER.

Things I have learned from
the life of Paul that have helped my life: _____

_____

_____

_____

_____

_____

Date: _____

_____

_____

_____

_____

_____

_____

Date: _____

_____

_____

_____

_____

_____

_____

_____

_____

_____ *Date:* _____

_____

_____

_____

_____

_____

_____

_____ *Date:* _____

"So the next generation would know them, even the children yet to be born, and they in turn would tell their children. Then they would put their trust in God and would not forget His deeds but would keep His commands."

PSALM 78:6-7

"One generation will commend Your works to another; they will tell of Your mighty acts."

PSALM 145:4

" 'These commandments that I give you today are to be upon your hearts. Impress them on your children. Talk about them when you sit at home and when you walk along the road, when you lie down and when you get up.' "

DEUTERONOMY 6:6-7

About the Author:

Roy Lessin is the co-founder of DaySpring Cards, and is presently the senior writer and editor for DaySpring. He is a graduate of Bethany School of Missions, where he received his ordination. He has served as a Christian Education Director in California, and as a missionary in Mexico and Puerto Rico. He presently serves as a Bible teacher, counselor, and seminar leader.

Other books by Roy Lessin include:
Forgiven
A Fruitful Life
A Mother's Heart—A Garden Place
Never Forgotten…Always Loved
Within His Hands…Without A Fear
Knowing His Best…Walking In Rest
Receiving His Blessing…Giving His Love

About the Artist:

Michael Dudash has been a professional artist/illustrator for the past 21 years. Since his education at the Minneapolis College of Art and Design, and the Macalaster College in St. Paul Minnesota, Michael has received a national reputation. His paintings have won him numerous awards from the Society of Illustrators, the Society of Publication Designers, and several publications. A Christian who happens to be an artist, Michael uses his abilities and talent to spread the Gospel of Jesus Christ through his paintings. His paintings are a thing of beauty and inspiration, but more importantly instill something greater in the viewer.

Other MasterPeace® Collection works:
Art Prints and Sculpture: Victorious Lion of Judah
Limited and open edition Art Prints:
The Journey
He Shall Hear My Voice
A Father's Heritage